Danes and their Politicians

Voters in Scandinavia · 2

THE ROCKWOOL FOUNDATION RESEARCH UNIT

Gunnar Viby Mogensen

Danes and their Politicians

A Summary of the Findings of a Research Project on Political Credibility in Denmark

AARHUS UNIVERSITY PRESS

Copyright: Aarhus University Press, 1993
Translated by Susanne Marslew, Thomas L. Jakobsen and Tim Caudery
Word-processed by the Rockwool Foundation Research Unit
Cover design by Poul Nørbo
Printed in England by the Alden Press, Oxford
ISBN 87 7288 451 7

AARHUS UNIVERSITY PRESS
Building 170
Aarhus University
DK-8000 Aarhus C, Denmark
Fax + 45 86 19 84 33

For a list of other publications by the Rockwool Foundation Research Unit, see page 83.

Contents

Preface

A recurring topic in Danish public debate is the relationship between the people of Denmark and their politicians. Many political commentators have noted an increasing level of public distrust in politicians, and several present and past MPs have also commented on this phenomenon. The sense of a crisis in public confidence is further fuelled by sensational headlines in the daily papers; the press appears to attempt to ferment a new political scandal almost every day.

Recently, the problem seems to have acquired additional momentum through the [first] referendum concerning the Danish ratification of the Maastricht Treaty. This, as all Europe knows, resulted in a narrow 'No'-vote, despite the recommendation to vote 'Yes' given by a clear majority of Denmark's political parties and the 179 MPs, by most of the nation's professional and industrial organizations, and by the labour unions.

In the light of these increasingly conspicuous signs of a crisis in public confidence, the Rockwool Foundation Research Unit decided that the subject of the relationship between the Danish people and their representatives in parliament, and in wider terms of the Danes' opinions of their political system in general, was sufficiently important to merit the setting up of a research project on the matter. (The Rockwool Foundation Research Unit is based at Danmarks Statistik, the Danish Central Bureau of Statistics. Over the past five years the organization has specialized in analyses of important issues in Danish society.)

The project was started in 1989, with most of the data collection being carried out in 1990 and 1991. The results obtained were subsequently published in April 1992 in two books: *Vi og vore politikere* (*We and Our Politicians*) and *Kan vi stole på politikerne? (Can the Politicians be trusted?)*. In the first of these publications the results were presented in detail, whereas *Kan vi stole på politikerne?*, which I prepared, was intended as a more accessible summary of the results.

The primary and well-defined scientific aim of the research was to discover how relations between the political system and the population have developed in Denmark. In addition, it was the desire of the Rockwool Foundation to make a contribution to a serious debate on Danish democracy.

This second aspect of the project is reflected by the inclusion of three polemical discussion papers in *Kan vi stole på politikerne?* These were written by Poul Hartling (a former Prime Minister of Denmark), Svend Jakobsen (a former Speaker of the Danish Parliament), and Erik Ib Schmidt (a former Head of the Treasury Department). These three men have all played central rôles in Danish political life.

Since the relationship of trust between people and politicians has generated interest and discussions in several other Western nations, it has been decided to publish this English-language text (based on a shortened version of *Kan vi stole på politikerne?*) as part of the final report.

During the work in the Unit, the researchers became aware of a controversy concerning the interpretation of Danish research about a related subject – namely the degree to which Danish voters are motivated by conceptions of the public interest as opposed to calculations of private economic interest. After termination of the main project we therefore asked one of the leading experts in this field, Dr. Douglas A. Hibbs, to undertake an evaluation of the results available for Denmark. The outcome of this research is presented in Douglas A. Hibbs' *Solidarity or Egoism?*

Finally, I should like to point out that the project about political credibility, like earlier projects undertaken by the Research Unit, has been carried out under conditions of complete scientific independence – even in terms of our relationship to the Rockwool Foundation. It would, however, have been impossible to carry out our investigations as extensively and as flexibly as we have without the great interest and support of the Foundation. I would like to mention especially the cooperation we have received from the Director, Bent Løber and from the present Chairman of the Board, Group President and Chief Executive Tom Kähler. Furthermore, I would like to take this opportunity to thank all the researchers and experts involved in the project, as well as our landlord, Danmarks Statistik, whose management team – headed by Hans E. Zeuthen – and employees have taken a great interest in the project.

A special word of thanks goes to my co-director Erik Ib Schmidt, who has, as always, made and followed through innumerable valuable suggestions for the production of this volume.

Gunnar Viby Mogensen, Copenhagen, August 1993

Part One: Analyses

1. Organization and Structure of the Project

The research project management team decided from the outset to use a dual structure for the investigation of confidence in politicians. First, a number of expert researchers were asked to carry out detailed studies within their particular fields, and second, a 'reference group' was set up to offer constructive criticism of the researchers' ideas and activities by means of discussion of proposals for data collection, delimitation of subject matter, etc.

The reference group included both research experts and experienced commentators on and participants in Danish political life. In the latter group, we managed to secure the participation of Poul Hartling, a former Prime Minister; Svend Jakobsen, a former Speaker of the Danish Parliament; and Erik Ib Schmidt, a former Head of the Treasury Department. As has been mentioned in the Preface, they all contributed polemical articles on the relationships between politicians and the public to the Danish edition of this book.

The 'expert' members of the reference group were recruited from the fields of political science, history, sociology and economics. Among them was Hans E. Zeuthen, head of Danmarks Statistik. The group of researchers also included a number of experts with interdisciplinary credentials: Jørgen Goul Andersen (Lecturer at the Department of Political Science, Aarhus University), Hans Jørgen Nielsen (Lecturer at the Department of Political Science, Copenhagen University), Niels Thomsen, (Professor at the Department of History, Copenhagen University), and Jörgen Westerståhl (Professor of Political Science, University of Gothenburg).

Working Hypothesis and Topic Area
The field of research for the research group was set out in the following definition of aims and working hypothesis formulated by the Research Unit:

The aim of the project is to shed light on the *relationship between politicians and the public in Denmark today*. This concerns both the communication of information, opinions and ideas between the two groups, and also their views on and reactions to each other. At times, this relationship appears to be marked by good contacts between populace and politicians, and by public confidence in politicians and in their ability to lead and govern. At other times, a 'credibility gap' arises – either in relation to the government or to particular political leaders and parties, or in relation to politicians and "the system" in more general terms.

The topics for research were similarly predefined. It had, for instance, been decided that all the main aspects of the changes in relationship between populace and politicians during the last decades should be examined within a broader historical framework covering developments in the political system (and in particular in the structure of the political system, see chapter 2) over an extended period of time. It was felt that this historical framework should preferably be studied all the way back to the introduction of constitutional democracy in 1849.

It had further been decided that an understanding of the changes in confidence relationship would be aided by an analysis of developments in media coverage of political topics and of politicians as people. However, despite generous funding from the Rockwool Foundation, limitations in finances meant that priorities had to be established, and so the work in the media field was centred around an analysis of Danish television coverage of political news. The choice of television was made in the light of the fact that roughly 50% of the respondents in other surveys have stated that television has a particularly strong influence on their political opinions and their perception of politics in general.

Since the topic of public opinion of politicians has many facets, a decision was taken to carry out *two* analyses on the main project topic – political credibility – using separate methods. One analysis used questionnaire-based interviews with a large and representative group of Danish citizens. The other used long and thorough talks (based on the 'casuistic' method) with a relatively small number of interviewees, all of whom had agreed to have these conversations recorded on tape.

Since the first of these recordings were found to provide new and surprising information, it was decided to extend the recorded interviews to a larger group of voters and also to a number of politicians and other experienced political commentators (journalists specializing in politics, etc.).

The Analyses
The main elements of the project may be summed up as follows (with the names of the researchers responsible):

– a relatively detailed historical analysis of the developments in the relationship between the electorate and politicians over the last 140 to 150 years, with particular emphasis on the political structure, as defined in chapter 2 of this book. This analysis, intended, among other things, to create a historical frame of reference, was carried out by Professor Niels Thomsen.

– an account of changes in TV coverage of political issues through detailed analyses of a substantial number of news broadcasts dating from 1965/66 and from 1990/91. The analyses, conducted by Professor Jörgen Westerståhl, aimed to show, among other things, whether increased distrust among voters might be linked to developments within the television medium.

– a survey based on approximately 2000 questionnaires concerning public perceptions of political credibility, what determines the public's attitudes towards politicians, and how attitudes have changed during recent decades. This survey was carried out by Lecturer Jørgen Goul Andersen.

– finally, the recording and analysis of a number of in-depth interviews with a smaller group of voters. In this case, the intention was to obtain a more detailed picture than the one provided by the questionnaire survey, and also possibly to substantiate the questionnaire findings. Lecturer Hans Jørgen Nielsen, who conducted this part of the project, additionally sought to discover how MPs themselves perceived their relationship with the voters. This aspect of the survey was again conducted through in-depth interviews, in this case with MPs from all the parties represented in Parliament. In the present volume, the findings from the interviews with MPs can be found in chapter 5, whereas results from in-depth interviews with voters appear in chapter 6.

The second part of this volume contains a summary of the polemical papers by Poul Hartling, Svend Jakobsen, and Erik Ib Schmidt.

Method
Though both the theme and the topic of the research project on political credibility were defined from the outset, the researchers carried out their work as independent investigators – both in relation to the outside world and to each other. Their work was, in other words, to be published as a series of individual contributions. At the same time, however, the researchers obviously had to be in continual contact with each other concerning their choices of

methods, types of data, etc. These contacts were formally coordinated through project meetings at the Research Unit at Danmarks Statistik.

The Concept of Constituency

In the following chapters a recurrent concept is that of *constituency*. The use of this term deserves an explanatory note:

In Danish political terms the concept of *constituency* has two interrelated meanings, a purely *political* and a formally *legal* one.

In its purely *political* sence a *constituency* means the groupings of voters appealed to by any politician or political party. These groupings usually are defined in terms of economic, trade or cultural interests and are invoked in the political debate as supporters of present or future policy.

This meaning of *constituency* is derived from its *legal* meaning in the context of the Electoral Act. In its present form, dating from March 31, 1953 with minor later amendments, this Act fixes membership of the Folketing (Parliament) at 179, including 2 representatives of Faroe Islands, and 2 for Greenland. All responsible citizens of 18 years of age or over have the right to vote.

The 175 members representing Denmark are elected by proportional representation in 3 divisions: Greater Copenhagen, Islands and Jutland, consisting of 3, 7 and 7 counties respectively. These counties are further subdivided into constituencies. 135 members of Parliament are elected to constituency seats, whereas the 40 remaining seats are distributed amoung the 3 divisions in such a way as to ensure representation of all political parties running for Parliament in proportion to their voter support, provided they poll at least 2% of the vote.

As candidates without party affiliation are rare, a candidate for Parliament is usually nominated by a political party to a certain constituency but runs together with that party's candidates from one whole county. In this way, no member of Parliament is elected by the voters in one constituency only but collects votes from the whole of the relevant county if not from the whole of Denmark, as the distribution of the 40 remaining seats determines the final result.

2. The Historical Analysis:
The Changing Roots of Danish Politics

This chapter outlines some major changes in the relationship between politicians and electorate in Denmark during this century. It tries to explain changes in political behaviour, including election results, and in recorded attitudes to politics and recorded levels of trust in politicians, by relating all these to changes in the political roots system. The material used includes data from the Danish Gallup Institute collected since 1944, survey data collected by researchers from the universities in Copenhagen and Aarhus during the ten national elections held in the period 1971–1990, and material from a number of more specialized survey studies on political behaviour and attitudes since 1975. Equally important, however, are the data and conclusions in a vast range of books and articles on modern Danish politics, social change, mass media, culture and public opinion.

According to the historian, Professor Niels Thomsen, the changes in political trust and distrust over the years since World War II can best be understood if one considers the Danish political structure as being in two sections. On the upper level are the political institutions – e.g. Parliament – defined in the constitution; and on the lower level are the political 'roots', i.e. party constituency organizations and various other special interest groups established by the populace. These popular organizations provide the means to fulfil the constitutional ideal of enabling the people to influence decisions made by political bodies.

The 'roots' are defined very broadly (see figure 2.1) as all political, professional, and ideological groups, the mass media, various institutions, and any places or occasions where social issues are discussed and evaluated. These roots thus range from party constituency organizations and political groups, professional and trade organizations, environmental conservation organizations, etc. to newspapers, publishers, radio stations, school classes, city hall meetings, canteens, discussions in pubs or over dinner, and TV viewing.

Figure 2.1. Explanatory model

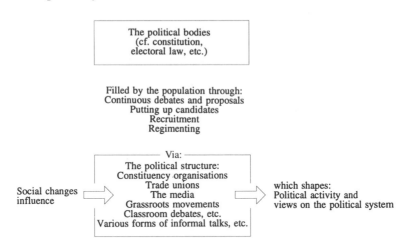

The political roots are very important to a democracy which has a system of elective representation. They provide the means for continual recruitment of new politicians and for the nomination of political candidates. They also provide the opportunity for an ongoing political debate which generates, among other things, a public respect for political decisions, and which permits the implementation by social means of political measures intended to effect social objectives.

Since the structure of the roots system is constantly changing – as a result of, among other things, changes in society, see figure 2.1 – it would be natural to assume that any development involving a weakening of the roots, or a deterioration in communications between the roots and the constitutional system, might partially explain an increase in voter distrust.

It is thus not unusual to find political systems which are functioning poorly, or perhaps even breaking down completely, because their roots have weakened, fossilized, or developed in an inappropriate way. Such developments can pose a threat to the stability of the political system itself. An obvious contemporary example of this is the political and social collapse in Eastern Europe and the former Soviet Union.

The Development of the Roots: A Story with Four Phases
The first Danish constitution of 1849 replaced one of the most autocratic forms of government in Europe. Niels Thomsen divides his analysis of the

evolution of the Danish political roots system since that date into four phases: 1849-1940, 1940-1960, 1960-1973, and finally 1973 to the present day.

The first Danish constitution – the June Constitution of 1849 – formed the legal foundation for the introduction of democracy to Denmark. The Constitution – the wording of which drew inspiration from the 1831 Belgian Constitution – took shape under the influence of both the 1848 Paris Revolution and a peaceful mass demonstration in Copenhagen, which addressed itself to the newly-installed and weak monarch, Frederik VII. The men behind the constitution were predominantly academics with liberal ideas.

The First Years: No Official Parties
In the years immediately following 1849, no political parties as we know them today existed. Political parties were by no means a necessary ingredient of the new political system; the Fathers of the Constitution systematically avoided the party concept in the constitutional text. They adhered to the politically liberal theory that the best decisions would result from ideas being put forward by individuals in Parliament. Furthermore, they wanted to avoid 'French conditions', i.e. the existence of very polarized political groups in Parliament. But over the next 20 to 30 years, ideological differences and class interests produced clear-cut groups in Parliament, with corresponding constituency associations behind them.

By the turn of the century, political life had crystallized into the so-called *'four-party system'* consisting of the Conservatives, the Liberals, the Social Democrats, and Social Liberals.

By the end of a thirty-year-long constitutional struggle, which resulted in the introduction of cabinet responsibility, the four parties were thoroughly organized. They had constituency organizations throughout the country, networks of party newspapers, youth groups, etc., and each party had established strong links with certain economic interest groups as well as with various cultural and educational institutions such as folk high schools (independent colleges):

-   The Social Democrats were closely linked with the powerful Danish trade unions and the labour cooperative movement
-   The Liberals had ties with the farmers' unions and most of the agricultural cooperative movement
-   The Social Liberals had ties to the budding smallholder movement as well as to sections of the intellectual and academic world in Copenhagen
-   The Conservatives had substantial backing from employers' associations,

trade guilds, and commerce in general, as well as from large-scale farming interests and the majority of senior civil servants and public employees.

The party system was essentially class based, so in the long run economic and social developments determined election results. Voter turn-out had already exceeded 75% by the 1880s, and the same level was reached by women and by all citizens between 25 and 30 years of age when these groups were enfranchised in 1915 and 1920 respectively. By then, it had become established practice that negotiations between social and economic interest groups were conducted within the parliamentary system by the four parties. Although severely tried by the depression of the '30s, this semi-cooperative system of parliamentary politics was so firmly entrenched that little headway was made by the new, extremist parties – the Communists and the Nazis. The four old parties jointly retained at least a 90% share of the votes cast at every election before 1940. And as none of the four parties ever achieved a parliamentary majority on its own, the political process was tied to a system of alliances and pragmatic deals, usually taking the interests of most major groups and professions into account.

The German Occupation and the Disruption of the Political System
The second phase in the development of the political roots covered the period from 1940-1960. It began with the German occupation of Denmark in April 1940.

Even though Denmark largely avoided the devastating effects of the war, the occupation shook established political routines. The four old parties formed a coalition government, which administered the country under German guidance until August 1943. That government then resigned, since a majority of the population were by then following the orders of the resistance movement, united in the Danish Freedom Council. People joined in protest actions and hid saboteurs on the instructions of the resistance. The Danish Freedom Council was a largely non-political body – only two very small parties, the Danish Communist Party and the Danish Unity Party, were represented on it. However, the old parties had to recognize Council and take it into the cabinet formed after the German surrender in May 1945, in response to the demands of both public opinion and of the victorious Allied Powers.

The excitement subsided quite soon. At the first post-war election held in October 1945, the Communist Party obtained 12% of the vote, thanks to the prestige it had gained through participation in the resistance movement. But the old parties still got 82.5% of the vote, and very soon things seemed very much back to the pre-war patterns. By 1950, the Unity Party was out of

Parliament, and the Communists again gained less than 5% of the votes cast. Still, the events of the occupation had shown the Danish people that they could make decisions within the framework of new groupings, and that they could act independently and without party guidance.

Party membership and electoral turn-out were high during the first post-war years, but then began to decline. In this and various other ways there was a progressive weakening of the hold on the political roots formerly possessed by the old parties.

Tabloid newspapers which cared little for politics gained readers at the expense of broadsheet national dailies. In the provincial press, the smaller party newspapers had to close down; those remaining came to concentrate on local news and entertainment instead of political issues, since most of their readers now belonged to parties other than that of the newspaper itself. Even the traditional party loyalties of various interest organizations became open to question.

The Danish radio company, which enjoyed a monopoly and was financed exclusively by licence fees, also contributed to a weakening of the control of the media formerly enjoyed by the parties. From around 1950 onwards it covered political news more closely, and it became more active in the political debate. The four old parties remained the central focus of its interest, but none of them could dictate the choice of political themes or the balance of political coverage, as they had done with the party newspapers. In addition, even new and small parties got a chance to present themselves to the public through the radio.

Student Revolt, Grass Roots Movements, and a 'Depoliticized' Press
Up until this point, no definitive shift had occurred in the fundamental political values of the system. Such a shift, however, was clearly apparent during the third phase (1960-1973), which in Niels Thomsen's analysis began with the general election of 1960. Many voters switched their support from one party to another in that election. In addition, there was a general shift of 3-4 % to the political left - an unusually large movement in Danish political terms. It was the result of the popularity enjoyed by the Socialist People's Party (SPP), founded in 1959 by an ex-chairman of the Communist Party. The Communist Party itself went into decline.

Shortly afterwards there arose the many grassroots movements of the 1960s, the student revolt of 1968, and a period of labour unrest and wildcat strikes. This period also saw unbroken further growth in the popularity of tabloid newspapers, and a continuous increase in the influence of television. During the sixties, TV came to hold large numbers of the population spellbound every evening. It became very influential in setting the political agenda, even at the parliamentary level.

The combined membership of the political parties dwindled from 22% to 12% of the total number of registered voters between 1961 and 1974, and the 12% remaining were increasingly untypical of the population – they were, for one thing, much older than the average.

Three referenda (on land ownership, electoral age, and the EEC) saw large groups of voters reject the recommendations of the parties which they had voted for at the last election, providing further evidence of the decline of party influence over public opinion.

At the same time, economic interest organizations began to adjust to the weakening of the parties – and in so doing accelerated that process. The organizations established their own groups of experts, who were able to negotiate directly with parliamentary politicians and senior civil servants. In other words, political favours and state subsidies were sought and negotiated outside the framework of traditional alliances and party loyalties. The tremendous growth of the public sector, and Parliament's ambitions in the area of social engineering, meant that organizations, firms, local groups, and private citizens all became used to making demands. They tended to see things only from their own narrow perspectives, and to be content to leave Government and Parliament to foot the bills for their requirements. One result was rapidly increasing taxes and rate of inflation, so that Denmark, together with other Scandinavian nations, set world records for taxation levels. Another consequence was that the social solidarity inherent in traditional welfare state attitudes was strained to breaking point. Among new voters, there was an evident lack of a sense of responsibility towards the democratic process.

Several of the phenomena mentioned above were also present in other Western European nations. However, Niels Thomsen stresses the point that in Denmark the reorganization was so radical that, in retrospect, it is evident that the basis of Danish political life passed a watershed in the 1960s. The earlier ties between voters and politicians lost much of their strength.

A Landslide Election
That new and controversial political trends had become established during the 1960s became evident at the 1973 election, which opened the last phase of the period being analysed. The 'landslide election' expressed a very powerful reaction against the established political system: no less than 43% of those who had voted at the last election switched their votes in 1973, and the four old parties and the SPP declined from a combined 93% share of the vote to 64%. Because of the low Danish parliamentary representation threshold of

only 2% of the national vote, the decline of the old parties permitted five new parties to enter Parliament. The largest by far was the Progress Party (PP), a curious version of extreme populist liberalism, which gained 16% of the votes. These votes were drawn from all sections of society, including even the working classes.

The election largely reflected the dissatisfaction of the 'silent majority' with the high Danish taxes, and with what the majority perceived as 'freeloaders' or 'social parasites'. But there was also widespread irritation with what was perceived as ever-increasing anarchy as represented by demonstrations, wildcat strikes, and housing squats. The Government, it seemed, was unable to control such activities – and the mass media revelled in covering them. Revolutionary ideologies and campus unrest spread within the universities, which had recently been expanded at an unprecedented rate. The traditional trade union leadership lost its grip on certain segments of the labour market, giving even the old Communist Party a second chance for a few years. But there seemed to be no common element to the signals being sent out from the grass-roots level – apart from discontent.

After some years of continuous turbulence, a more orderly pattern of party politics has been more or less restored, but on a new basis. The voters have neither been pacified nor permanently polarized. Acceptance of and belief in the democratic system is even more general in Denmark than in other EEC countries. But 10 to 20% of the voters now change party allegiance between elections, and only some 6% of the electorate are paid-up members of a political party. Organizations and newspapers do not lend automatic support to a particular party, and at referendum time, voters rely more on mass media and each other than on politicians. The repercussions of 1973 have permanently undermined the voters' trust in their politicians. These developments can be seen from figure 2.2.

The political leaders have had to face the fact that the number of core voters committed to each party is decreasing. Consequently, the successful political leader must address marginal voters, and must do so in a way which ensures television coverage. He no longer plays the rôle of advocate or shop steward in the elective democracy, enjoying lasting confidence and understanding from supporters; instead, he must act like a salesman, or like an agent employed by voters on a temporary basis until a new agent offers a better bargain.

The rôle of politicians and the grip of the political parties on public opinion, which were modified but not fundamentally changed by the experiences of the war years, underwent lasting changes as a result of important developments in the 60's – developments in the social structure, media patterns, etc., and the expansion of the public sector. These political changes were reinforced by the economic recession unleashed by the oil crises of 1973 and 1979, which the politicians were unable to do much about. The powerlessness of politicians to act in the oil crises was brought about in part by the fact that so many voters changed sides at elections, and thus rendered Parliament very inefficient. Though some aspects of the economy have improved markedly since 1982, and political instability is less apparent, voters have remained cautious and alert, giving only provisional support to political leaders.

Figure 2.2. The population's evaluation of the politicians and the Danish political system.

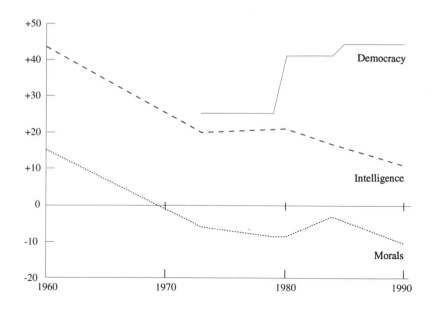

Note: Attitude to democracy: Positive minus negative percentages, 5 year average, Eurobarometer (1973-1989)
Evalution of the politicians: Moral and intelligence:
    Percentage of 'higher than the population'. Gallup (1960, 1973, 1984, and
    the average of two measurings in 1991).
Source: Niels Thomsen's contribution in *Vi og vore politikere.*

A Weakened Root Structure

One can conclude that the traditional political root system was markedly weakened by the social and political changes of the 60s, with much influence and popular interest being transferred instead to grass-roots movements and to the media. The outcome was a transformation of the connecting links between politicians and voters. Where formerly the relationship was one of trust, authority and group solidarity, it has changed to the cruder, weaker and less stable relationship of a political market system.

It is important to note, however, that while this change clearly weakened the performance of the political system, it did not reduce people's belief in democracy – nor, for that matter, in the other basic human and social values. On the contrary, these beliefs now appear to be more fixed and less manipulable.

3. Television and Politicians

In his analysis of the media, which centres on an analysis of television, Professor Jörgen Westerståhl – who is well-known for, among other things, his extensive chronological studies of the selection and presentation of news in different media – begins by pointing out that Danish broadcasting, like many other Western European broadcasting systems, followed the BBC model from the outset. This implied that public broadcasting should not only eschew all ties to parties and organizations but also that it should, as far as possible, avoid controversial approaches to news reporting. The reporting could be described as strictly factual, and 'official'.

During the late 1960s, however, the revolutionary movements among young people and students influenced Danish intellectual circles considerably, as pointed out in chapter 2. The impact on Danish broadcasting was strong. A new form of investigative and critical journalism developed. According to the new ideology, the activities and statements of all those who held power in society should be critically scrutinized. The journalists in the Watergate affair became rôle-models.

As a result, much power over the media was transferred from outside to within the media; and there, too, there was a transfer of power, from the owners and editors to the journalists. This meant the influence of government and political parties on Danish broadcasting decreased.

Influence of the Media on Public Opinion
The substantial current influence of television is documented in the project's comprehensive interview survey, in which 70% of the respondents named TV news broadcasts as a central source for their information and opinions about political matters. The corresponding percentages for national broadsheet and tabloid newspapers were 35 and 9% respectively.

Thus, there was felt to be good reason to concentrate research on TV's main news programme (TV-Avisen), and to select for study one recent period and one from the early days of the programme, before the youth and student revolts. Such a comparison, it was thought, might say something about television's contribution to the current distrust in politicians.

In order to make sure that the comparison covered periods with important political issues on the agenda, four-month periods during which the finance bill was in passage through Parliament were selected for 1990/1991 and 1965/1966. Through video recordings and news-reader scripts, over 2100 items of domestic news in the main evening TV news broadcasts of the two periods were examined.

The news items were classified according to two criteria: *subject matter* (politics, business, accidents etc.) and *character* (positive, neutral, or negative news items). The category 'politics' was broadly defined, and included not only news of government, parliament and local government, but also all other news where politics and politicians were mentioned. The distinction between positive and neutral news is, as has often been observed, difficult to make, and the two categories were therefore combined. Negative news, which ever since the age of the first daily newspapers seems to have played a crucial role, was divided into two subgroups. One subgroup was 'criticism', typically covering features in which a journalist – or more frequently a person from outside the media – criticizes people, proposals, measures, or states of affairs for which someone might be considered personally responsible. The subgroup 'other negative news' was for events like crime, accidents, social and environmental problems, etc.

The results are shown in tables 3.1 and 3.2 below.

Table 3.1. Four months of domestic TV news in 1965/66, classified according to subject matter and general character.

| Subject matter | General character | | | |
	Positive/ neutral	Criticism	Other negative	Total news
Politics	302	35	19	356
Administration/ organization	238	17	73	328
Business	53	4	17	74
Culture, etc.	37	0	0	37
Accidents/crime	0	0	200	200
Other	357	2	34	393
Total	987	58	343	1,388

Table 3.2 Four months of domestic TV news in 1990/91, classified according to subject matter and general character.

Subject matter	Positive/ neutral	General character Criticism	Other negative	Total news
Politics	123	145	30	298
Administration/ organization	9	4	5	18
Business	59	36	40	135
Culture, etc.	34	1	0	35
Accidents/crime	0	10	65	75
Other	122	31	60	213
Total	347	227	200	774

The figures can be summarized in five conclusions:

1) The proportion of political items among the domestic news items has increased by about 50% during the past 25 years. Political news now accounts for nearly 40% of all domestic news.
2) Conversely, the number of non-political items has been substantially reduced.
3) The proportion of 'critical' items in domestic news has increased dramatically. Whereas in 1965/66 the distribution of items under the headings 'positive/neutral', 'critical', and 'other negative' was 71, 4, and 25% respectively, the corresponding figures were 45, 29, and 26% in 1991/92.
4) The proportion of critical items has increased particularly with regard to politics or politicians. Thus, about 50% of the TV news items on politics or politicians now involve criticism, as against 10% in 1965/66.
5) Finally, approximately 65% of all critical domestic items concern politicians and politics. Another 16%, incidentally, concern representatives of the business sector.

Confrontational Journalism
Westerståhl's summary is that the outcome of the developments of the last 25 years can be described as *confrontational journalism*. Its structure leads to a

never-ending search for combatants. These can be most readily recruited from among politicians and representatives of special interest organizations. Westerståhl does not claim that Danish journalists are alone in using this form of journalism, which in fact prevails throughout the Western world; but he stresses that Danes have apparently taken the genre further than is the case in most other countries. In Westerståhl's view many of the 'interviews' with former and present ministers, mayors etc. recorded during the 1990/91 period can almost be described as brutal interrogations.

A Special Study of the Finance Bill
The general conclusions presented are supported by a more detailed study of the reporting on the finance bill, and by statements made in survey interviews by the various party spokesmen on financial affairs. The politicians declare that issues where there is conflict dominate far too much in TV reporting, while too little time is devoted to the content of the bill and to thorough and detailed coverage of the various parties' standpoints and proposals.

As can be seen from the figures below, the suggestion that there is heavy emphasis on the reporting of conflicts is supported by a quantitative analysis.

	Issue	Decision-process	Alia	Total
1965/66	33	36	31	100
1990/91	19	45	36	100

The share of features related to special issues has thus decreased significantly from 1965/66 to 1990/91, whereas the political game surrounding the Finance Act, with all its potential conflicts, has been upgraded. The impression of a reduction of interest in factual information was further supported when Jörgen Westerståhl moved on to a qualitative analysis of relevant features. The language used in reporting the bill was less precise in 1990/91 than in 1965/66. Moreover, the general presentation of the content of the finance bill, as broadcast on the TV news for November 26, 1965, was lacking in 1990. Thus, the heavy concentration on the conflict perspective is seen to be at the expense of more substantive information.

Final Assessment
In his final assessment of the changes in TV news coverage of politics, Jörgen

Westerståhl stresses that the 'tabloid trend', combined with a focus on reports on conflict, has some other serious consequences:

Society adjusts. Because criticism evidently sells well, politicians as well as other public figures become 'media-ized'. They adapt themselves to the media priority of reporting conflicts.

Voters get tired. Politicians no longer appear as people making responsible decisions on important social issues, but as a group of people who are perpetually quarrelling and fighting – they run around 'like fools', as it was put in a TV news item in 1990.

If the picture of Danish politics presented by television were correct, the level of conflict in politics should have gone up *massively* during the last 25 years, but absolutely nothing points to that having happened. Jörgen Westerståhl therefore draws the conclusion that TV news broadcasting has in fact – through its priorities, choice of topics, and journalistic bias – contributed to the decreased level of trust in Danish politicians.

4. Public Trust in Politicians in 1991:
A Questionnaire-Based Survey of 2,000 Danes

In studying trends in changes in the political root structure, we noted a considerable decline in public trust in politicians in the early 1970s – a decline which was reflected in the results of the 1973 election. But what is the situation like in the early 1990s with regard to voters' trust in their MPs and the decisions they make? Has the dramatic decline in trust continued since the early 70s?

As will appear from the following, the answer depends very much on how one defines the word 'trust'. Accordingly, the Rockwool Foundation Research Unit considered the question of what is implied by the terms 'trust' and 'distrust' in politicians. They also considered how, when a well-defined meaning of 'trust' had been established, different levels of trust among different groups of the population could be explained, as well as changes in attitudes over a period of time.

Jørgen Goul Andersen's analysis of these matters is based on the project's large questionnaire-based survey conducted in the spring of 1991 among a representative group of approximately 2,000 adult Danes. In addition, data from other selected surveys conducted in recent years have been used when possible.

To begin with, Jørgen Goul Andersen points out that statements such as '30, 60 or 90% of the population now distrust politicians' should be viewed with considerable caution. For one thing, voters are often all too ready to declare themselves to be in agreement with negative statements about politicians. Secondly, concepts such as trust and distrust are very complex, involving a variety of elements.

If researchers set out to study possible changes in the public's degree of trust in their politicians, they must therefore ask more concrete questions concerning a number of aspects of trust/distrust. For example, one could ask about people's confidence in politicians making correct decisions, or their trust in the moral standards of politicians. If changes within a number of such interrelated aspects point in the same direction, it may then be meaningful to talk about a change in the level of public trust in politicians.

The Relative Extent of Distrust

By going through all the available Danish studies on the subject, Jørgen Goul Andersen was able to produce a list of statistics dating from 1971 up to the present day. These data show the changes in public confidence in politicians generally making the right decisions for the country – what we could call a pragmatic aspect of trust.

Deducting the percentage of those disagreeing with the view that politicians usually make the correct decisions from the percentage of those agreeing, we end up with a figure expressing the 'balance of opinion'. A high positive score for this balance of opinion thus shows much confidence, whereas a low score is an indication of distrust. The results are shown in Figure 4.1.

Figure 4.1. Confidence in Danish politicians, 1971-1991: Confidence in politicians making the right national decisions. Balance of poll: bias towards confidence.

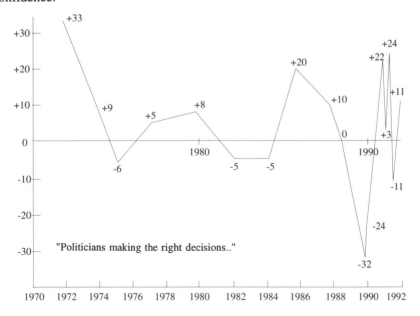

Note: Confidence in the politicians: 'As a rule one can trust politicians to make the right national decisions'. Balance of poll denotes percentage of 'agree' minus percentage of 'disagree'.
Source: Jørgen Goul Andersen's contributiution in *Vi og vore politikere*.

The figures are generally lower in the period after 1973 compared to the period before, but they do fluctuate quite substantially, and often over short periods of time. Consequently, it is hardly safe to argue that there is any stable, long-term trend in the series of figures covering the period from 1973 to 1992. What can be stated – and this is supported by various other occasional surveys that have been carried out during the period – is that:

- the degree of confidence in the decisions made by the politicians is not as high as the level preceding the 1973 landslide election;
- the last years of the 1980s saw a particularly deep confidence crisis, which has apparently still not been overcome; and
- these factors suggest a long-term trend of a gradually decreasing level of trust. This stands out clearly when the period before 1973 is compared with later periods, and somewhat less clearly when only the last two decades are considered, since these represent a period of large and perhaps increasing fluctuation in the level of trust in politicians.

It can also be said that the era of voters 'looking up to politicians' has quite clearly passed.

It may be further added that Jørgen Goul Andersen's analyses of public trust in the moral fibre of politicians (as expressed through various measurements of people's views of politicians as being opportunistic) and of public opinion as to whether politicians are sufficiently aware of and receptive to voters' views quite distinctly indicate decreasing trust during the period after 1973.

Measurements of these three central aspects of trust thus all support the theory that the long-term trend in public trust in politicians is downward, with 1973 as a definitive turning point. If, moreover, public confidence in Parliament is compared with the reliance placed on other groups and public persons, Parliament rates very low today, and they also rated low ten years ago. So too, incidentally, do major businesses and the daily press.

The Limits of Distrust
Do the opinion polls conducted for this project and others, then, suggest that the decrease in confidence in politicians is an indication that democracy is in jeopardy?

Jørgen Goul Andersen's analyses show this to be far from the case. There appears to be a considerable level of satisfaction with the current system of parliamentary democracy. The proportion of Danes satisfied with their political system is clearly above the average of most other EEC countries.

According to several surveys using different formulations of the question, 60-80% of Danes claim to be content with the structure of the Danish democracy (see table 4.1)

Table 4.1. Evalution of the functions of democracy 1973-1989.

	1973-79		1980-84		1985-89	
	EEC	DK	EEC	DK	EEC	DK
very contented	7	10	8	17	6	16
reasonably contented	43	50	42	48	43	48
reasonably discontented	29	27	29	27	31	26
completely discontented	14	9	15	6	13	5
Balance	-½	25	-2	42	-2	45

Note: The balance represents the predominance of positive percentages (contented) against negative (discontented); very/completely count as double. Average of measurings in Oct/Nov the year in question.
Source: Eurobarometer no. 32, Dec. 1989

A still greater proportion of the population want the existing elective democratic structure to be retained, rather than having a system of more direct democracy. Measurements taken over long periods of time show that the balance between supporters and opponents of a transition to more referenda remains unaltered. In 1991 there was also a clear majority opposed to having more parties in Parliament. It was felt by the majority that the present admission threshold of 2% of the votes cast is low enough.

Furthermore, the idea of a strong leader assuming control in the event of an economic crisis appeals to a decreasing number of Danes. In 1973, 56% of the interviewees saw some justification for such firm control of decision-making; in 1991 this number had dropped to 30%. It should be pointed out, however, that the surveys did not make clear whether the 'strong leader' was to be one who had been asked to assume control for a certain period of time, or whether he had seized power.

Finally, Jørgen Goul Andersen shows that the proportion of Danes professing allegiance to a particular political party has remained unchanged since 1971, despite the decline in actual party membership. This is an indication that the parties still have firm roots among the general population, even though this fact is now more rarely manifested through membership of local political organizations.

Reasons for the Distrust

The research which has been conducted in Denmark and abroad during the last decades has suggested two issues as being at the heart of our distrust in politicians. Some results have indicated that distrust is particularly strong among the socially disadvantaged, who through their feelings of resignation have become politically apathetic. Some researchers have designated this phenomenon 'political alienation'. Other and more recent results have pointed instead to political beliefs as the crucial factor. According to this theory, distrust will be particularly strong among groups who feel inadequately represented politically.

Jørgen Goul Andersen's analysis of the reasons for differences in distrust among different groups of voters therefore attempts to answer a really central question: how does political belief compare with social and political resources in explaining differences in distrust?

Concerning social resources, the analysis shows education, job and employment sector (private versus public) to be particularly significant in relation to the feelings of trust or distrust in politicians expressed by voters. The most marked sense of distrust is to be found among the more poorly educated members of the electorate, among blue-collar workers and among the unemployed. Thus it seems that being socially weak or strong does play a significant rôle.

The analysis, however, shows an even greater effect related to political beliefs, in that large numbers of voters expressing distrust also turn out to feel that their opinions are not represented at all in the political process. The results display the predicted effects of whether voters feel in touch or out of touch with the government in office, and close to or far from the parliamentary centre. Not surprisingly, voters who support the opposition parties feel more distrust, as do voters favouring the political extremes.

Furthermore, however, the analysis shows a surprisingly strong effect related to specific ideological views which cut across existing party ideologies. These are views on foreigners (meaning refugees and immigrants) and attitudes to the EEC.

On both these issues, current Danish policy is at present supported by rather large majorities in Parliament, and often by the left and right alike; in other words, support for these policies traverses the political spectrum. Nevertheless, the survey shows that as many as 44% of the voters want Danish aid to the Third World to be cut by half, and 42% are of the opinion that unemployed immigrants should be sent home. 46% of the voters who expressed an opinion in the survey either wanted Denmark to leave the EEC or to be integrated to a lesser degree than that required by the Single European Market.

Figure 4.2 shows clearly that this feeling of not being properly represented politically by MPs on these (often quite emotional) issues causes distrust.

Figure 4.2. General confidence in the politicians, divided according to the degree of aversion to immigrant subsidies and the attitude to EEC integration. Balance of poll: confidence predominant. Percentage.

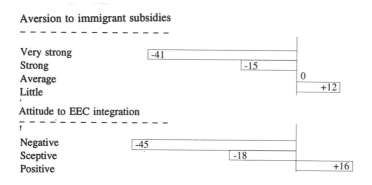

Source: Jørgen Goul Andersen's contribution in *Vi og vore politikere.*

In the figure, a horizontal column to the right of the zero-line denotes trust in the politicians, whereas a horizontal column to the left denotes distrust. The further left the horizontal column extends, the greater the distrust. As can be seen, the level of distrust is by far the greatest among those groups who are opposed to giving financial support to immigrants and/or are negatively inclined towards further integration into the European Communities. In other words, a marked relationship between *internationalization* and distrust is suggested.

Jørgen Goul Andersen supplements his conclusion by arguing that the strong effect of the unwillingness to pay money to foreigners and of negative attitudes to the EEC goes hand in hand with the fact that these opinions appear to be held most often among the socially less advantaged. Today, such viewpoints are largely 'suppressed' by most political parties and to some extent by the media as well. The result is that these opinions cannot but lead to feelings of increased distrust in politicians.

5. Parliamentarians' Views on Distrust

As mentioned in the introduction, the Rockwool Foundation project included interviews with a number of key people in the Danish Parliament. One of the objectives of these interviews was to obtain a picture of the awareness among the politicians themselves of feelings of distrust, and to discover how close their contact to the electorates and their political roots really is.

Hans Jørgen Nielsen chose a relatively open format for the interviews. The discussions did cover the following set items, however:

- the question of whether the distrust issue is really a problem, and whether politicians are aware of it in their contacts with voters;
- relationship with fellow MPs;
- relationship with professional and industrial bodies, the press, local councils, etc; and finally
- the use made of the party organization.

The politicians were selected with the intention of covering the maximum possible spread of views. Consequently, all parties were represented. There were MPs from both rural and metropolitan areas. Both senior and junior MPs were chosen, and there were MPs with and without experience of high political office. It was made quite clear that the politicians would *not* remain anonymous in the research project's publication of the results. Edited versions of the tape recordings were distributed to all participants for information and for the correction of potential misunderstandings. However, the final summary of results presented here remains, obviously, the responsibility of the researchers and the project team.

A State of Harmony

No interview-based survey of this type had ever been conducted in Denmark before. Hence, many of the findings came as a surprise to the researchers and the general public alike. It was particularly surprising that in many ways the analysis disclosed generally harmonious working practices among MPs.

Consider, for instance, relations between MPs. Most interviewees told of widespread cooperation, with relationships of great openness and trust existing between politicians. A left-wing politician thus felt quite able to ask advice on housing matters of a right-wing politician who happened to be an estate agent; and, furthermore, did so in the full expectation that the advice given would be detailed and accurate. A newly-elected conservative was able to tell of a similarly positive experience: during committee work she was warned by a socialist against accepting a compromise for which she would be unable to obtain support from within her own group.

Other interviewees explained that if they or their deputies are unable to attend a committee meeting, they can rely on getting unbiased reports not only from parties with whom they are generally in agreement, but also from opposing parties – even from those on the far political wings.

A few interviewees even argued that cooperation across party barriers can be easier than working with one's closest allies. One MP puts it this way:

Your own party is special in that, that is where your competitors are. People who are your friends one day may not be so the next. And information you entrusted them with yesterday may be used against you today.

But given the very high-minded and proper nature of inter-party cooperation, how did the politicians themselves explain the critical opinions of the electorate? A great number of the politicians interviewed agreed on a basic explanation: the image of politicians presented to the voters is markedly different, and the politicians bear part of the blame for this themselves. As soon as they have an audience – for example, when television covers a debate in Parliament – a different note is sounded.

The Liberal MP Bertel Haarder, the former Minister of Education, puts it this way:

Of course distrust exists, for the very reason that many politicians – almost as an occupational disease – believe that they can best advance their own interests by generating distrust – distrust in the prime-ministerial candidates of other parties, distrust in proposals put forward by other parties, distrust in other parties' analyses of issues. No wonder people speak ill of politicians, considering the way they talk of each other.

Some politicians stated that what was hardest to come to terms with as an MP was the discrepancy between everyday dialogue and cooperation on the one hand, and the formal attacks on political opponents in parliamentary debate and in the media on the other.

Contact with Organizations

How are contacts with other, ever more powerful organizations perceived? On this issue the survey presents a similar picture of harmony and cooperation. As a rule, politicians consider organizations to be good partners in parliamentary work, and the normally tranquil cooperation that goes on between politicians and organizations is characterized by the same atmosphere of openness and trust as exists among politicians themselves. This at any rate is the case while the work going on is not visible to the general public.

Therefore, virtually all Hans Jørgen Nielsen's interviews with politicians tell of fruitful cooperation with the organizations, who, among other things, often provide high-quality, comprehensive information to politicians prior to parliamentary debates of bills.

The politicians seem to accept information given in briefings by organizations with caution. They constantly bear in mind that organizations do not always represent all the opinions of all their members. And the politicians interviewed were convinced of their ability to see through organizations' motives. One MP, for instance, divided the organizations into two groups, as did several other politicians in the survey:

One group is made up of the lobbyists, who clearly aim to control my opinions, and who will try to pull the wool over my eyes on issues I know little about. The other group consists of professional and industrial bodies who very definitely take political realities into account from the outset. They will state their case if they are dissatisfied about something, but they will also acknowledge my political standpoint and try to negotiate. That is what I call proper discussion, political relationships based on mutual trust.

Here again considerable weight is placed on the importance of mutual trust behind the closed doors of Parliament.

When Hans Jørgen Nielsen attempts to open those doors by inquiring about the politicians' own perceptions of their contacts with the electorate, his immediate impression is that politicians admit to encountering criticism from voters, but not personal distrust. But perhaps the politicians meet but a few, selected, and thus positively-oriented voters?

Contacts with Voters

Hans Jørgen Nielsen's analysis of politicians' contacts with their voters involved asking the politicians themselves about the matter, and then double-checking their statements by comparing them with the results of the project's questionnaire survey of over 2,000 Danes, in which this subject was also dealt with.

When discussing voter contact, the politicians generally claimed to enjoy relatively close contacts with a surprisingly large number of voters.

The contact was closest in non-metropolitan areas. In particular, those provincial politicians who had been born and raised in their constituencies had very close contacts with their electorates. These contacts consisted partly of the systematic and organized cooperation between the MP, local politicians and the constituency organizations, and partly of daily, informal contacts between citizens of the constituency and the politicians in question.

A Social Democrat MP, born and bred in his constituency, gave this account:

People knew me personally. They might ask me how my father was doing, or tell me about my children's activities. Once elected in a city in which you have spent all your life, you become part of its life... When I came home at night, somebody would often be waiting for me, or there would be 5 or 6 phone messages. Everybody knew where I lived and what time I arrived home on the train. In the course of a year I would thus manage to talk to thousands of people. My children refused to go with me into town, because we never got any further than to the pedestrian precinct before somebody would come up to me and say, 'I would like you to know...' or 'Couldn't you talk to...?'

A number of local politicians – both from the MP's own party and from others - have confirmed this description as being nothing less than the literal truth.

Several provincial politicians also told how their local municipal councils, political organizations and professional and industrial bodies maintained close contacts with their MPs in order to promote local political interests in Parliament. Since constituency organizations have great influence on who is elected to Parliament, it is often the case that the normal political groupings in Parliament are supplanted by groupings from specific areas of the country. This can happen, for example, when issues such as the prioritizing of infrastructure projects, decentralization, or the abolition of state institutions are debated.

This picture of close, daily contacts between voters and politicians varies to some extent, however. The interviews suggest stronger contacts in provincial areas than in Copenhagen, where – as one politician suggested – people are frequently unaware of which constituency they live in. The fact that the local newspapers in Copenhagen take only limited interest in politics is also of significance.

DANES AND THEIR POLITICIANS

Another point of detail is that the contact network is, as a rule, more easily maintainable for Social Democrat politicians. Social Democrats are numerous in every constituency; MPs for smaller parties are forced to cover several electoral districts. Furthermore, the Social Democrats enjoy the active support and assistance of the many elements that make up their movement, over and above the party constituency organizations: trade unions, local government politicians, the youth movement, etc.

Voter Contact seen Through the Voter Survey
The results of the extensive questionnaire-based survey confirm that the politicians' assessment of the extent of their contact with the electorate is to be trusted. It appears from the 2,000-odd questionnaires that no less than 15% of voters had spoken to a MP within the previous three years, and that 17% had attended a meeting at which a MP spoke. Some respondents had, of course, done both, but nevertheless 25% of the voters surveyed had been in contact with a MP in one way or another within a span of merely three years. A still greater number of voters – 43% – had had some contact with a local politician.

Thus the politicians do reasonably well in comparison with the grassroots movements, whose close connections with the populace are often stressed in both Denmark and the rest of Europe. According to another survey, 31% had taken part in some sort of grassroots activity over a similar period of time.

So, the politicians have a fairly extensive contact network. They meet a large minority of the voters, and those voters do not – the survey shows – differ radically from other voters in terms of attitudes. And since the politicians avowedly have great trust in one another and in the professional and industrial bodies, one might then ask whether the MPs feel that the sort of media coverage they get is so negative that it may account for the distrust that exists?

The Politicians' Opinions of the Press
The interviews with the MPs soon showed that the majority were of the opinion that at least part of the explanation of the increasing level of distrust lies here. In their assessment of media coverage, the politicians criticized one point which in many ways corresponds to the conclusions put forward by Jörgen Westerståhl in his analysis of television news broadcasts in chapter 3. The politicians generally felt that accounts of the facts in political issues were less frequent today than ten or twenty years ago. Instead, the media tend to focus strongly on the sensational aspects of the political game. Criticism – often personal criticism – is also more frequent. One politician argues that

'the press is only interested in conflict, thereby distorting the image of the Danish Parliament. The press contributes to a lowering of people's opinions of Parliament, and in turn to an aversion to political issues'. Another politician mentions the 'sensationalist bias of the media', and yet another argues that the distrust really exists in the media rather than among the general public.

Other people stress the emergence of an information problem. This is evident particularly to politicians appearing on TV. One description of the problem went as follows:

The task of the press has also changed. Today we do not have a forum, as we did in the early days of democracy, where you can stand up and present your goals, the means that exist for achieving those goals, and what the various perspectives of the situation are. The four paper system was one example of such a forum; another was the community centre meetings. Neither exists any more. Now that the old forums have gone, the press should – while retaining a critical attitude towards the Government – take on the task of informing people as well. It often happens nowadays that a statement which was part of a larger argument is presented out of context in the media, and as part of a kaleidoscope of political statements from different sides. The entertainment value is what counts.

The problematic relationship between politicians and the media may – as Jörgen Westerståhl stresses in his analysis – be partially explained by the fact that the press operates on self-determined, independent, journalistic basis. If the established channels of debate – the four paper system and electoral meetings – have disappeared without the press and TV having taken on the task of disseminating information and stimulating debate, we seem to have found a significant reason for the decreasing trust in our politicians.

But are there other reasons – apart from that admitted to by the politicians, that their tendency to project a confrontational image and to use and abusive language may break down public respect?

The Politicians' Own Experiences of Distrust

When Hans Jørgen Nielsen stopped discussing contact with voters and relations with organizations and the press, etc. with the politicians, but instead tackled the issue of the politicians' own experiences of distrust head-on, he was given both summaries of voter complaints and also a few tentative explanations of the phenomenon.

The reproaches made to politicians were particularly concerned with specific political decisions (as often as not irrespective of whether the politician's party had voted for or against the decision) and with the breaking of electoral pledges (irrespective of whether the party in question would or would not have been able to secure the parliamentary support necessary to fulfil the promises). Politicians were, in other words, seen as one breed, and electoral pledges were seen as promises that should be fulfilled, even if no one party had gained the parliamentary majority that would enable them to carry out those promises.

The broad explanations offered of the increased level of distrust pointed especially to the greater present-day complexity of the Danish Parliament, with its many parties and - until January 1993, where a majority government was established - its permanently unclear distribution of responsibility between minority governments and Parliament. In addition there is the increased complexity of the Danish society, partly resulting from increased immigration. When, at the same time, the media fails to establish a strong political channel for information to pass between government and the governed, society stands at great risk of being manipulated by people or organizations offering simple and readily comprehensible messages.

6. The In-Depth Interviews

The final part of the main analysis consisted of Hans Jørgen Nielsen's in-depth interviews with 23 voters. These people were selected from among the subjects of the large questionnaire-based survey; they were chosen with the aim of obtaining the largest possible spread of characteristics. Although it cannot be claimed that this was strictly speaking a representative group of Danish voters, the selection did cover all the various combinations found of political views and feelings of distrust in politicians, etc., and the group also displayed a range of characteristics in terms of sex, age, geographical area of residence and voting record. The aim of this part of the project was to obtain a more detailed picture than that which could be obtained from the restricted range of response options available on the questionnaire. It was also the intention to check the reliability of the questionnaire responses. Hans Jørgen Nielsen wanted particularly to follow up some apparently contradictory responses made to items on the questionnaire. Both in the survey for this project and in previous research on the subject, it has been found that many voters express conflicting views in their responses to a single questionnaire.

Politicians' Good and Bad Qualities
To start the discussion off, interviewees were asked to list some good and some bad characteristics of politicians.

Negative points were readily produced: 'None of them are credible'; 'They appear unable to take a global view'; 'They seem to lack the ability to cooperate'; 'Very often they change their ideas after an election', and so on.

When the interviewees were asked to list good points, silence typically ensued. When prompted again for a response, people sometimes added a few more items to the list of bad characteristics.

The question did succeed in providing a catalogue of the problems. It was also interesting that a number of bad qualities did not appear in the list. Politicians were never described as ignorant or incompetent; it was basically their willingness to act, not their ability, that was criticized.

In trying to isolate the recurring features found in the interviews concerning the bases for the distrust felt, the degree of political interest, etc., Hans Jørgen Nielsen found it useful to group the interviewees as far as possible. The groups he identified can be illustrated by the following five typical brief profiles:

The working class woman is unskilled, and is married to a blue-collar worker from a provincial town. She has little confidence in the system generally. Her attitudes are characterized by distrust; this distrust goes hand in hand with a lack of political interest. Her distrust is directed generally at all representatives of society. And despite inclining towards the Social Democrats more than any other party, she has little confidence in them, saying that the party 'will probably break its promises'.

The teacher, on the other hand, is interested in 'green' politics. He has most sympathy with the political left. He has his own opinion of politicians, based on his carefully-considered attitudes to life. On a number of issues he is critical towards the policies pursued, but he retains a general confidence in the politicians, who have, after all, been elected by the populace.

In *the sales manager*, who is politically conservative, one does not find a strong overall philosophy of life, as one does in the first two character sketches. Instead, there are features which have also been identified in the work of other researchers. Political attitudes are governed by events in the individual's private life rather than in society at large – with, in this case, problems with housing taxation being the most immediate issue.

In the case of the female *case officer*, it is observations of society at large (related to an active interest in politics) which control her outlook. That outlook is a highly sceptical one. She thinks that politicians ought to aim for 'objectivity' and 'breadth of view', but that they fail to do so.

Finally, there is the middle-aged and wealthy *businessman*, a member of a party with conservative values. He is interested in politics, even if he is not active in the party constituency organization. To him the crucial issue is the ability of politicians to make carefully-considered decisions and to resist pressure from interest groups. In his opinion, however, far too many politicians have shown themselves susceptible to pressure – particularly during election campaigns.

The interviews with the people described in these five miniature profiles with confirmation from the other interviews indicate that:

– though specific answers in the questionnaires were often contradicted during the long interviews, the overall impressions gained from the questionnaire survey concerning political interest and political distrust were confirmed. In this respect, the results obtained from the question-naires were correct.
– the answers concerning politics and politicians varied significantly from

voter to voter. There is no such thing as the definitive voters' verdict upon the credibility of the Danish politicians; instead, almost as many opinions were found as there were interviewees.

- the cogency of each interviewee's answers varied a lot. Where coherence exists, it seems that this may be the result of a conscious political philosophy, as in the case of the 'teacher' and to some extent the 'case officer'. It may also, however, be the result of more concrete individual experiences. Finally, in some instances views are so incoherent that one is led to suspect an ideological dilemma.

The 'Christmas Present' Dilemma

This dilemma resembles what Swedish researchers have labelled the 'Christmas present paradox': presented with the choice between better hospitals and a trip to Majorca, a Swede will choose both.

It seems from the analyses above that the Danes would do much the same. Hans Jørgen Nielsen asked the interviewees whether Danish politicians and parties ought to present more clearly delineated and differentiated images of themselves by, for example, being more precise in defining their visions of a future society, or whether politicians should instead seek compromises and focus more on cooperation. He also asked whether the parties should stick to pre-election promises after elections, or whether politicians should carry out 'the correct policy', even if this was unpopular with the electorate. The answers called for stronger political profiles as well as compromises and cooperation. Quite often the same interviewee would want both. Equal inconsistency was evident when people were asked to choose between responsiveness to the desires of the electorate and the need to make sound decisions. Hans Jørgen Nielsen points out that this two-sidedness – 'the Christmas present paradox' – was also evident in the large questionnaire-based survey. There was a majority in favour of parties being responsive to the wishes of the electorate, but a different question produced a majority in favour of compromises, even if this would mean that a party had to break electoral promises.

The Overall Picture

Hans Jørgen Nielsen rounds off his two analyses – one concerning MPs and one concerning the electorate – with the conclusion that the ability to get rid of incompetent rulers is at the heart of the democratic system. The creation of a certain critical attitude towards the politicians is thus a more or less natural product of the democratic structure. Political debates, analyses by the press, and election campaigns all have this effect. We Danes – unlike the citizens of many other countries – are accustomed to keeping an eye on our politicians. Therefore it was perhaps not so surprising that many interviewees were lost for words when urged to say something positive about politicians.

In many cases, however, statements and evaluations suggested double standards. An interviewee would strongly advocate cooperation, then a moment later would call for a greater degree of differentiation between the parties.

What was even more important was the fact that the voters often spoke about 'objectivity' and making the right decisions while emphasizing the importance of a contact between politicians and voters. Once again it seems that a parliamentary democracy requires a balance.

None of these problems would exist if Denmark had a one-party system - even if that situation would certainly generate other problems, as Eastern Europe has recently reminded us. The problems may thus be largely attributed to the fact that Denmark is a democratic state – and perhaps also to the fact that we currently have too little active participation in the political system – through the schools, through the media, and through our society in general.

Part Two: The Polemical Papers

7. Poul Hartling:
Does Our Political System Encourage Trust?

Former Danish Prime Minister Poul Hartling begins his paper by stating that his participation in the project's reference group has proved exciting and thought-provoking. He has a positive opinion of the project, and believes that it is of relevance and interest to the public.

At the same time, an apparent paradox presents itself: a large majority of voters have effectively renounced any direct influence on the selection of parliamentary candidates. This is left to the parties and their paid-up members. In most cases, the politicians criticized are nevertheless re-elected; and if they are not, it is not because of any criticism of them personally. Still, there is much talk of distrust in or even disgust with politicians. This implies a lack of consistent or logical thinking by voters. But perhaps another conclusion might be that what the term 'distrust' *really* represents is probably discontent with the policies pursued.

In general, Poul Hartling calls for a cautious interpretation of the signs of distrust emanating from the public. There has always been a tendency to criticize politicians with whom one disagrees. A number of opinion polls indicate that what is expressed by voters is discontent with the Government on the part of the Opposition's supporters, as well as vice versa. This pattern appears to hold for successive governments, regardless of their political complexion. All governments receive much criticism from their opponents, but this cannot really be defined as mistrust. It is discontent with and an attack on an opponent. And one may well then ask if criticism is in fact such a bad thing in a democracy.

Furthermore, Poul Hartling points to a number of aspects of political studies which in his opinion call for constant caution in the interpretation of results. For example, he points to the fact that interviews cannot be carried out 100% objectively, and also that the social sciences will always have to generalize to some degree, and that in doing so many important nuances are lost. Poul Hartling particularly warns against regarding politicians as a homogeneous group, as expressed in the term 'politicians': 'It has become customary – and not just among researchers – to talk of "politicians", disregarding the fact that this group consists of markedly different individuals and with widely differing opinions.' Finally, Poul Hartling suggests that scepticism is appropriate when, for example, one survey from March 1991 shows a high level of confidence, whereas a more recent survey from June 1991 shows lower figures than in 1971.

These reservations do not, however, induce Poul Hartling to deny that today political credibility is lower than it was a generation or two ago – and basically he sees the conclusions of the research project as being balanced and sound.

When considering the causes of distrust, Poul Hartling agrees with many of the theories put forward in the analytical part of the project. For example, he points to the increased proportion of women working, which has resulted in fewer women having time and energy to take part in political activities. A further change during the period has been that today many young couples do not subscribe to a daily broadsheet newspaper, and consequently get their political information through radio or television and perhaps a tabloid paper.

Poul Hartling mentions other factors. He particularly stresses the frequent confusion which often surrounds political decision-making as a result of the existence of minority governments throughout the '80s and the beginning of the '90s. In his opinion, the parliamentary system instituted in 1901 has suffered greatly in recent years. It has become customary that 'a majority outside the Government' can lay down national policies and control legislation. In a parliamentary democracy the voters might justifiably ask: 'What *is* a "majority outside the Government"? Is it not the very basis of parliamentary democracy that the majority should be *in* Government?'.

Poul Hartling blames this state of affairs on the opposition as well as on the Government. The Government has not been willing to take up even issues of importance in Parliament. The Opposition parties might be able to agree in imposing a policy on the Government which it does not want, but they have not been able to get a vote of censure through. This procedure is, not surprisingly, confusing and frustrating to voters and politicians alike - and it poses a threat to democracy.

Poul Hartling concludes by stating that:

- the survey shows that democracy in itself is not the object of distrust;
- an amendment to the constitution is not something which should be considered at present; and
- parliamentary democracy is fundamental to the Danish democratic system, and a parliamentary democracy requires mutual trust between voters and the elected politicians in order to function.

8. Svend Jakobsen:
Political Credibility in Denmark

Svend Jakobsen, former Speaker of Parliament, agrees with the belief that the public's trust in politicians has clearly deteriorated – this being a view which he himself put forward when he resigned from the post of Speaker. He believes that the Rockwool Foundation's analyses and conclusions should be closely read and discussed in all corners of the political world.

Svend Jakobsen furthermore points out that the basis of political life in Denmark has changed fundamentally without the political system keeping pace – and that this can explain much of the distrust. Likewise, the party political pattern has changed. But the changes within the party structures and working methods, as well as those in the more formal political structures and decision-making methods, have been far less dramatic than the changes in society. Consequently, there is a need for a considerable adaptation to the new realities by politicians and political parties alike.

So in his paper Svend Jakobsen focuses on a number of suggestions for reforming politics and the political system. He argues that it must be of vital interest to all parties to forestall a widespread revolt among voters.

As for the press, Svend Jakobsen believes that the new confrontational style of journalism is responsible for much of the increased distrust. With the demise of the party political press, nothing remains to balance the caricature of the political scene and its personalities that is presented in the Danish press of today. Svend Jakobsen argues that, in future, the press must live up to its proper rôle as critic in a democracy, by shifting its focus towards providing more fair and objective background information. The rôle and responsibility of the press in society should therefore be the subject of discussions between politicians and the leaders of the press. According to Svend Jakobsen, these discussions are so urgently needed that it would be natural for the Prime Minister – as Minister for the Press – to take the initiative in this matter.

Apparently, voters have been greatly disappointed by gaps between political pledges during election campaigns and subsequent political decisions. To overcome this, Svend Jakobsen argues that politicians have a duty to educate the electorate, by making clear that political views expressed represent ideals and ambitions, but that actual political decision-making is always shaped through discussions and debate. Politicians could also stress that their parties cannot promise to effect particular policies unless they win 90 of the 179 seats in Parliament.

New working methods should also be introduced, making it easier for the voters to find out who makes the decisions, and what they decide. The best way to achieve this would be to return to a situation in which Government can rely on a regular parliamentary majority. This would enable the government to do what the Constitution expects it to do, i.e. to rule and govern the country. In debates on future amendments to the constitution, one important proposal should therefore be considered; namely, a proposal that a majority in Parliament should support the formation of any government and furthermore that a parliamentary vote should indicate a majority in favour of the political programme put forward by any potential government. And even before embarking on such a possible amendment of the constitution, the politicians should strive to form governments on the basis of a regular parliamentary majority.

With regard to the working methods of political parties and their position in relation to the general public, Svend Jakobsen calls for, among other things, a strengthening of local party organizations, to be effected through increased decentralization of decision-making in the public sector. The parties must also consider methods of selecting candidates which will involve the electorate more actively. Furthermore, the system of devising party platforms which lay down precisely what views party members should espouse on every conceivable issue is surely outdated. This kind of party discipline belongs to the past; it does not suit the more independent character of the modern voter.

Finally, Svend Jakobsen discusses the significance of the EEC in the growth of public distrust. He is of the opinion that the EEC has had a certain impact in this respect. For instance, the Rockwool Foundation surveys show a greater trust in local politicians than in more distant decision-making bodies, including the EEC. Given the ever-increasing internationalization of society, it will become vital to find new ways of promoting discussions between politicians and voters regarding the decisions which are made jointly with other countries.

Svend Jakobsen puts forward a number of suggestions on how to reduce the distrust in democracy brought about by EEC-related factors. For one thing, he believes that the burgeoning EEC bureaucracy must be restricted in its size. Information on decisions and the decision-making should be open and accessible to everybody. The public should no longer be told that we make decisions for ourselves, for the fact is that Denmark only shares in the process of decision-making and is then obliged to pass the resolutions into Danish law. Everything must be brought out into the open on this matter. It is obvious that in order for the EEC to function, important decisions have to be made in cooperation with the other EEC-countries – and that Denmark may be outvoted, even on important matters. Finally, Svend Jakobsen calls for a strengthening of the democratic controls within the EEC, through increasing the power of the European Parliament.

9. Erik Ib Schmidt:
The People's Trust – Our Strength

Erik Ib Schmidt, former Head of the Treasury Department, begins his paper with an interesting discussion on the making of the June Constitution of 1849, shedding new light on this important historical chain of events. The uncertainties concerning the transition from nearly 200 years of despotism to some sort of representational democracy which surrounded the processes of shaping of the Constitution are reflected in its submissive references to royal power, though these are in effect of only academic significance. The document which is the very foundation of the political system thus presents a discrepancy between form and content, inducing Erik Ib Schmidt to – rather ironically – ask the question: 'Is not even the Constitution to be trusted'?

Erik Ib Schmidt then proceeds to discuss what he calls 'the undemocratic section of the Constitution'. He refers to section 56, which states that MP's do not have to answer to the electorate, but to their consciences alone.

The reasons for including this section, which has survived all revisions of the Constitution, are not mentioned in contemporary sources. But through his historical analysis Erik Ib Schmidt establishes that it was most probably because the constitution was framed by a small and select group – and that this élite group harboured a considerable distrust in the populace in general, as was also evident in the first electoral regulations. In true conservative fashion, these gave the vote only to males over 30 with no criminal convictions and who 'had set up house': in other words, to landowners. And to completely eliminate the risk of 'mob rule', section 56 was included, emphasizing as it did the gap between the electorate and the elected.

Today, however, the section appears an anachronism – partly because in reality few MPs can disregard their political hinterland. Nevertheless, Erik Ib Schmidt finds the section objectionable. As shown by the Rockwool Foundation surveys, the voters very much want politicians to be responsive and to make an effort to consider the interests as well as the views and sentiments of the electorate. 'To put it mildly, the section can be seen as displaying an authoritarian attitude on the part of politicians. More bluntly, one might ask whether the 1849 constitution was aiming for a true democracy, or for a sort of parliamentary absolutism'. This was the system which, according to Erik Ib Schmidt, developed over time into a system of rule by political parties.

Part of Erik Ib Schmidt's historical analysis deals with the development of the party system. This did not come into existence immediately after the introduction of democracy, but it soon took shape both in Parliament and, in the form of constituency organizations, in the rest of the country.

As is apparent from the analytical part of the project, the importance of the parties has, however, been reduced. Erik Ib Schmidt mentions the powerful interest groups, which have taken us in the direction of a system of corporate power, and the establishment of the media as an independent power in the political world.

However, Erik Ib Schmidt warns against oversimplified explanations of the problems the political parties have encountered since World War II. The reasons for the problems are highly complex and have not yet been fully explored. The Rockwool Foundation project has shown, perhaps to the surprise of many, that there is no basis for talk of a general crisis in trust in the political parties. Two thirds of all voters regard at least three of the parties favourably. It is as yet unclear what further developments there will be in the problems of the various parties in terms of, for example, falling membership. Nor is it clear what steps the parties can take to revive their organizations and create viable organizational structures. According to Erik Ib Schmidt, there is no doubt that a majority of the electorate would be dissatisfied with changes which led to:

- parties being sustained only by large subsidies from interest groups and companies
- active politicians being increasingly recruited from interest groups
- relations between politicians and voters being increasingly controlled by the media.

Finally, Erik Ib Schmidt also stresses the necessity of a return to more viable governments, i.e. governments with a substantial majority in Parliament. He argues that this is so urgently needed that a reform of the existing parliamentary system would be an obvious step to take in a future amendment of the constitution. Without majority governments it will hardly be feasible to deal effectively with one of the most serious problems of society, one that must invariably give rise to distrust in politicians and the political system: 'We cannot go on for years with 300,000 on unemployment benefit and at least 400,000 people unemployed in the sense that they would like to have some sort of paid job suited to their qualifications, age and physical condition'. This is a very clear warning that unemployment causes distrust and poses a threat to democracy.

Appendices

Figure 2. The percentages of voters in party organizations, 1935–1991

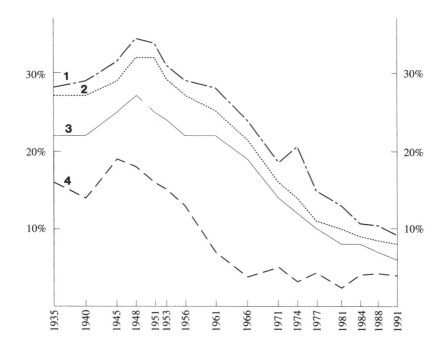

The three broken lines show the numbers of members of the parties' constituency associations as percentages of the votes cast for those parties at an election in the same year (or as percentages of the average number of votes cast for those parties at elections in the preceding and following years).

The unbroken line shows the number of members of all political associations as a percentage of the total number of votes cast at the parliamentary elections in question.

Reading from top to bottom:

1. Membership of the four old parties
2. Membership of all parties
3. Membership of political associations as a percentage of the total number of votes cast.
4. Membership of new parties.

Source: Niels Thomsen in *Vi og vore politikere*

DANES AND THEIR POLITICIANS

Table 1. The influence of various mass media on voters' attitudes to political questions. Figures are given as percentages of the total number of respondents (N=2056)

	Has great signifi- cance	Has some signifi- cance	Has a little sig- nificance	Has no sig- nificance/ irrelevant	Total of 'great' and 'some' sig- nificane
Television Channel 1	30	40	20	10	70
Television Channel 2	24	39	24	14	63
National Radio	24	34	25	17	58
Tabloid newspapers	2	7	16	74	9
Other national newspapers	14	21	14	51	35
Local daily newspapers	9	24	20	46	33
Periodicals	6	18	17	58	24
Discussions with others	24	35	22	19	59

Source: Jørgen Goul Andersen in *Vi og vore politikere*

Table 2. Proportion of the electorate who have spoken to MPs, divided up according to parties supported.

	A*	B*	N=
ELECTION of 1990:			
Voter's party			
Christian People's Party	18	13	40
Centre Democrats	21	1	87
Social Democratic Party	22	8	614
Progressive Party	27	4	78
Social Liberal Party	29	8	69
Conservative People's Party	30	7	260
Socialist People's Party	32	3	178
Liberal Democratic Party	33	15	280

*A   Percentage of voters who have spoken to a MP directly or who have attended a meeting at which a politician spoke

*B   Percentage of those who voted for a party who are members of that party

The figures in column A are derived from the mass survey section of the project. The membership percentages in column B are based upon information from the parties.

Source: Hans Jørgen Nielsen in *Vi og vore politikere*

Table 3. Items on the main national evening news on TV Channel 1, October 1 1990 – January 31 1991, classified according to subject matter and character.

Figures as percentages.

Subject matter	Items of different character classified according to subject matter				Subject matter categories classified according to character			
	Pos/ neu- tral	Cri- tical	Other nega- tive	Total	Pos/ neu- tral	Cri- tical	Other nega- tive	Total
Politics	35	64	15	39	41	49	10	100
Economy	2	–	–	1	100	–	–	100
Crime	–	1	23	6	–	6	94	100
Accidents	–	3	10	3	–	27	73	100
Industry	17	16	20	17	44	27	29	100
Social matters	3	2	6	3	35	19	46	100
Environment	1	4	6	3	20	36	44	100
Technology	4	–	2	3	74	5	21	100
Health	5	7	10	6	33	26	41	100
Administration/ organizations	3	2	2	2	50	22	28	100
Denmark – abroad	10	1	6	6	68	6	26	100
Culture	10	–	–	5	97	3	–	100
Various	10	–	–	6	100	–	–	100
Total	100	100	100	100	45	29	26	100

Number of items: 774

Notes:
– The study covers domestic news items and also international news where Denmark or Danes were involved.

– The field 'Politics' is widely defined. It includes not only items directly concerning politicians or political parties, but also items where politicians are mentioned or criticized in relation to events in the society in which politicians were not the main actors.

– Defining the 'character' of the news involves classifying news items according to the standard categories of positive, neutral and negative news. Positive and neutral news are here combined into one category, and negative news involving critical statements is separated from other negative news.

Source: Jörgen Westerståhl in *Vi og vore politikere*

Table 4. Items on the main national evening news on TV Channel 1, November 24 1965 – March 24 1966, classified according to subject matter and character.

Figures as percentages.

Subject matter	Items of different character classified according to subject matter				Subject matter categories classified according to character			
	Pos/ neu- tral	Cri- tical	Other nega- tive	Total	Pos/ neu- tral	Cri- tical	Other nega- tive	Total
Politics	31	60	6	26	85	10	5	100
Economy	3	–	1	3	94	–	6	100
Crime	–	–	30	7	–	–	100	100
Accidents	–	–	28	7	–	–	100	100
Industry	6	7	5	5	72	5	23	100
Social matters	2	–	1	2	85	15	–	100
Environment	–	–	4	1	24	–	76	100
Technology	2	–	–	2	100	–	–	100
Health	3	1	3	3	71	3	26	100
Administration/ organizations	24	30	21	24	73	5	22	100
Denmark abroad	3	2	1	2	85	12	3	100
Culture & various	26	–	–	18	100	–	–	100
Total	100	100	100	100	71	4	25	100

Number of items: 1380

Notes: See table 3.
Source: Jörgen Westerståhl in *Vi og vore politikere*

Table 5. Voters' opinions of the political debate. Percentage of respondents agreeing with each opinion (more than one response could be given by each respondent).

Question: Which of these descriptions do you think apply best to present-day political debate?

Focuses on individuals	68%
Of poor quality	39%
Superficial	37%
Malicious	32%
Constructive	4%
Friendly	4%
Dignified	3%
Objective	2%

Source: Sonar/*Morgenavisen Jyllands-Posten* 23.6.1991

Table 6. Aspects of trust in the morality of politicians. Percentage horizontally.

	Agree completely	Agree to some extent	Neither agree nor disagree/Don't know	Disagree to some extent	Disagree fully	Balance of opinion/trust
People who want to reach the top within politics will have to abandon most of their principles.	18	32	23	16	10	-24
Politicians normally say what they mean	6	26	16	30	22	-20
There is a large gap between the election promises of politicians and their actions after they have been elected (Observa)		77	8	15		-61
A politician maintains a standpoint – until he takes a new one (Observa)		71	9	20		-51
Politicians are more concerned about being re-elected than about solving the political and economic pro-blems of the country (Observa)		66	10	24		-42
MPs earn too much (Observa)		43	22	35		-8

Note: Observa = Observa poll in *B.T.* (9.12.1990). The Observa figures were split up according to party allegiances. The distribution of replies for the entire population has been estimated on the basis of the distribution of votes at the election.
Source: Jørgen Goul Andersen in *Vi og vore politikere*

Table 7. Evaluations of the responsiveness of the politicians (1991). Percentage horizontally.

	Agree comple- tely	Agree to some extent	Neither agree nor disagree/ Don't know	Disagree to some extent	Disagree fully	Balance of opinion/ trust
Generally, politicians give too little con- sideration to the opinions of voters.	30	32	20	14	4	-44
Generally, politicians have a good idea of what ordinary people think.	5	24	22	26	23	-20

Source: Jørgen Goul Andersen in *Vi og vore politikere*

Table 8. Evaluations of the intelligence and moral standards of politicians as compared to the general public, 1960–1991. Figures as percentages.

	1960	1973	1981	1984	1991
The intelligence of politicians compared to that of the public:					
- Higher	48	30	25	24	18
- The same	48	60	71	69	75
- Lower	4	10	4	7	7
The moral standards of politicians compared to those of the public:					
- Higher	21	10	8	12	7
- The same	73	74	76	73	72
- Lower	6	16	16	15	21

Note: Percentages calculated exclusive of those responding 'do not know/do not want to answer'. The studies from 1960-84 have been made available by AGB Gallup. Number of respondents in all surveys: approximately 1,000.
Source: Jørgen Goul Andersen in *Vi og vore politikere*.

Figure 3. Proportion of voters agreeing that it would be sensible to let a 'strong man' seize power in an economic crisis situation, 1971–1991. Balance of opinion shown in percentage points.

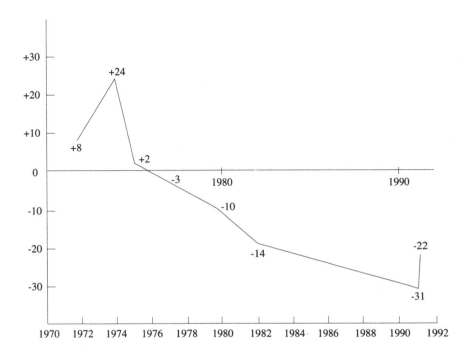

Question: 'Do you agree that it would be very sensible to let a strong man seize power in an economic crisis situation?'
Source: Jørgen Goul Andersen in *Vi og vore politikere*

Table 9. Social background and political trust. Figures given as balances of opinion or as deviations from average index values.

	General trust (balance of opinion)	Trust in practical decisions	Trust in ethics (balance of opinion)	Trust in responsiveness to voters	(N)
Men	+ 1	.10	-23	.17	876
Women	-13	-.08	-25	-.14	999
Age in years:					
15-19	+ 4	.18	- 3	.50	103
20-29 -	-10	-.06	-22	.23	359
30-39 -	-6	-.13	-26	-.12	356
40-49 -	-	-.04	-30	-.02	353
50-59 -	+ 2	.24	-22	-.02	234
60-69 -	-11	.15	-30	-.17	244
70+	-13	-.05	-24	-.20	226
Education level:					
7–9 years of schooling	-12	.05	-29	-.25	882
School leaving examination or 10 years of schooling	-	.05	-20	.01	624
High school examination or equivalent	+ 3	-.16	-22	.63	369
Employment:					
Blue-collar workers	-17	-.13	-34	-.44	384
Salaried employees (lower grades)	+ 2	.06	-20	.28	510
Salaried employees (higher grades)	+15	.09	-30	.82	142
Independent farmers	+38	1.45	+ 7	.84	40
Other self-employed persons	-	-.05	-15	.00	74

Annual income, DKK:					
0–149.999	−14	.00	−26	−.08	921
150–199.999	− 6	−.17	−25	−.18	345
200–249.999	+ 4	.18	−25	.19	207
250.000 +	+21	.18	−31	.73	201
Employment sector:					
Private sector	+ 4	.24	−23	.18	667
Public sector	− 5	−.10	−28	.05	433
Not in employment	−15	−.14	−24	−.17	775
Eta coefficients:					
Sex	.07*	.03	.01	.08*	
Age	.05	.05	.07	.10*	
Education	.08*	.03	.04	.17**	
Employment	.13**	.09**	.09**	.17**	
Income	.12*	.04	.03	.14*	
Employment sector	.10**	.07**	.03	.08**	
Percentage of variance accounted for (R2):	3.4	2.2	1.8	6.4	

Notes: The Eta coefficients show the strength of the correlation. Statistically significant correlations are marked *. Correlations marked ** are statistically significant when the other variables are taken into account (a multiple classification analysis – MCA analysis – has been made, the other results of which are not shown in the table). The 'percentage of variance accounted for' figures refer to an analysis of the correlations between education, employment, employment sector and mistrust made for persons in employment.

Source: Jørgen Goul Andersen in *Vi og vore politikere.*

Figure 4. Political distrust in Denmark (unbroken line) and Sweden (broken line), 1968–1991. Percentage of respondents agreeing that politicians take too little account of voters' opinions.

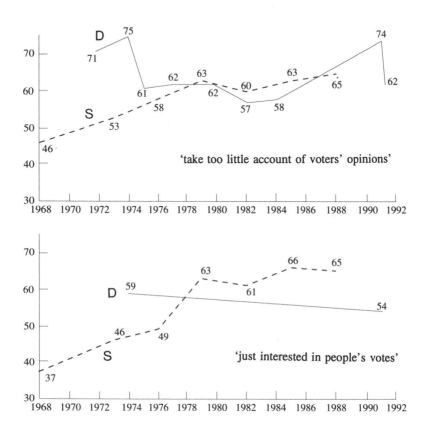

(1): Sweden: 'Those making decisions in parliament take little account of what ordinary people say and believe', Denmark: 'In general, politicians take too little account of what the voters say'

(2): Sweden: 'The parties are only interested in people's votes, not in what they think', Denmark: 'The political parties are only interested in my vote, not in what I think'.

Sources: Gilljam & Holmberg 1990

Table 12. The proportions of members of the Danish Parliament belonging to various socio-economic categories, 1966 and 1988. Expressed as percentages.

	1966 Members of Parliament	1965 The electorate	1988 Members of Parliament	The elec-torate
Blue-collar workers	10	27	6	21
Salaried employees	63	19	76	31
Self-employed	23	15	15	7
Others	4	39	3	41
Totals	100	100	100	100

Note: The group for comparison is for 1965 the entire population aged 20 and over, and for 1988 the entire population aged 18 and over. In 1988 the unemployed were included in the category 'Others', but this was not the case in 1965. Students are counted in the appropriate categories. In 1988, the unemployed amounted to almost 6% of the population aged 18 and over.
Source: Henrik Christoffersen in *Vi og vore politikere, Statistisk Årbog (The Statistical Yearbook)* and *Statistiske Efterretninger (Statistical Information).*

Table 13. The proportions of members of the Danish Parliament from various employment sectors, 1966 and 1988. Expressed as percentages.

	1966 Members of Parliament	The electorate	1988 Members of Parliament	1987 The electorate
Agriculture, fishing	17	15	9	6
Trade, crafts, industry	13	51	14	38
Education	17	4	25	7
Social and health services	3	6	6	16
Defence	2	1	3	2
Others	48	23	43	31
Totals	100	100	100	100

Note: The group for comparison (the electorate) is based entirely on those in paid employment.

Source: Henrik Christoffersen in *Vi og vore politikere, Statistisk Årbog (The Statistical Yearbook),* the 1965 Census and *Nationalregnskabsstatistik 1989 (National Budget Statistics, 1989).*

Table 14. The proportions of members of the Danish Parliament from the public and the private employment sectors, 1966 and 1988. Expressed as percentages.

	1966 Members of Parliament	1967 The electorate	1988 Members of Parliament	1987 The electorate
Public sector	36	19	54	35
Private sector/no sector	64	81	46	65
Totals	100	100	100	100

Note: The group for comparison (the electorate) is based entirely on those in paid employment. The figures for 1967 are approximate.
Source: Henrik Christoffersen in *Vi og vore politikere* and *Statistisk Årbog (The Statistical Yearbook)*.

Table 15. Ages of Danish MPs, 1996 and 1988. Expressed as percentages.

	1966 Members of Parliament	1966 The electorate	1988 Members of Parliament	1988 The electorate
Under 40	12	37	12	43
40-49	29	20	46	18
50-59	35	18	27	13
60 +	24	25	15	26
Totals	100	100	100	100

Note: The 1966 electorate were all over 20, and the 1988 electorate were all over 17.
Source: Henrik Christoffersen and *Statistisk Årbog (The Statistical Yearbook)*.

Table 16. Sex of Danish MPs, 1966 and 1988. Expressed as percentages.

	1966		1988	
	Members of Parliament	The electorate	Members of Parliament	The electorate
Women	11	51	31	51
Men	89	49	69	49
Totals	100	100	100	100

Note: The 1966 electorate were all over 20, and the 1988 electorate were all over 17.

Source: Henrik Christoffersen and *Statistisk Årbog (Statistical Yearbook).*

Table 17. Levels of education of Danish MPs, 1966 and 1988. Expressed as percentages.

	1966	1988	
	Members of Parliament	Members of Parliament	The electorate
Trained in a trade, or without education leading to any special qualification	51	33	86
Higher education	49	67	14
Totals	100	100	100

Note: The group for comparison (the electorate) is for 1988 all those aged 20-67 years. It is not possible to obtain comparable data for 1966.
Source: Henrik Christoffersen and *Statistisk Årbog (Statistical Yearbook).*

DANES AND THEIR POLITICIANS

Figure 5. Ages of members of the Government, 1966-1987.

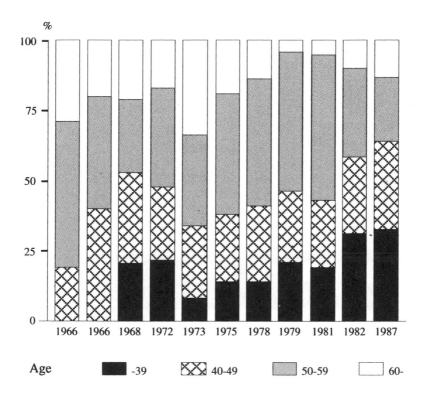

Source: Henrik Christoffersen in *Vi og vore politikere*

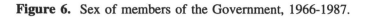

Figure 6. Sex of members of the Government, 1966-1987.

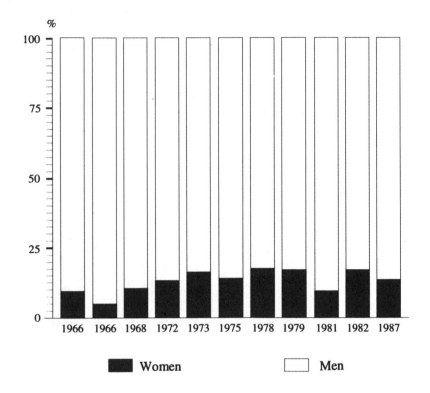

Source: Henrik Christoffersen in *Vi og vore politikere*

Figure 7. Level of education of members of the Government, 1966-1987.

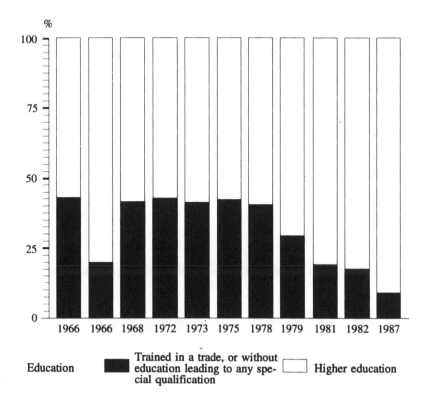

Source: Henrik Christoffersen in *Vi og vore politikere*

Figure 8. Socio-economic groups of members of the Government, 1966-1987.

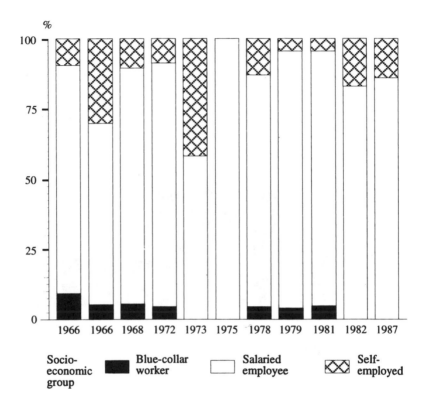

Source: Henrik Christoffersen in *Vi og vore politikere*

Figure 9. Employment sector of members of the Government, 1966–1987.

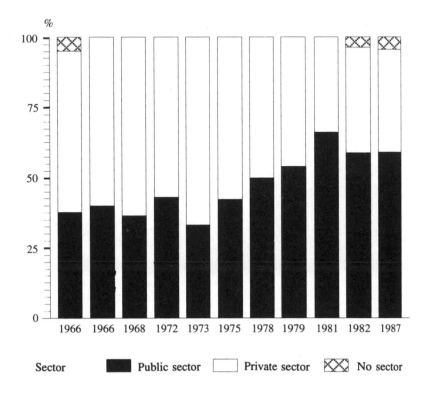

Source: Henrik Christoffersen in *Vi og vore politikere*

Figure 10. Payments to MPs, top managers' income levels and the average income level, 1967–1989.

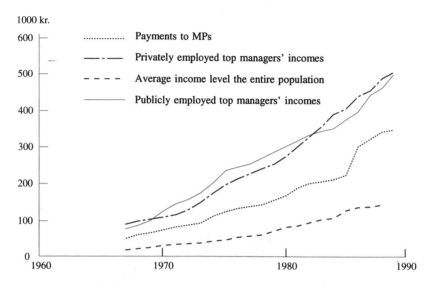

Source: Henrik Christoffersen

Figure 11. Payments to MPs compared with income levels for other groups and the average income levels 1967–1989.

Relatively

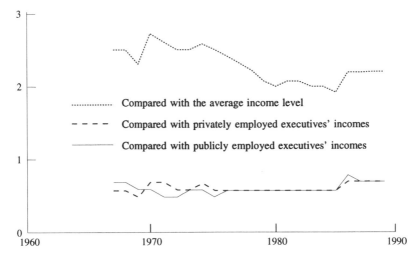

Compared with the average income level

Compared with privately employed executives' incomes

Compared with publicly employed executives' incomes

Source: Henrik Christoffersen

Index